MONSTERS & MYTHS
CLASSICAL MYTHS

By Gerrie McCall and Lisa Regan

Gareth Stevens
Publishing

Please visit our Web site, www.garethstevens.com. For a free color catalog of all our high-quality books, call toll free 1-800-542-2595 or fax 1-877-542-2596.

Library of Congress Cataloging-in-Publication Data

McCall, Gerrie.
 Classical myths / Gerrie McCall and Lisa Regan.
    p. cm. — (Monsters & myths)
 Includes index.
 ISBN 978-1-4339-4994-4 (library binding)
 ISBN 978-1-4339-4995-1 (pbk.)
 ISBN 978-1-4339-4996-8 (6-pack)
 1. Animals, Mythical. 2. Monsters. I. Regan, Lisa. II. Title.
 GR825.M264 2011
 398.24'54–dc22

                                              2010033447

Published in 2011 by
Gareth Stevens Publishing
111 East 14th Street, Suite 349
New York, NY 10003

Copyright © 2011 Amber Books Ltd, London

Illustrations copyright © Amber Books and IMP AB

Printed in the United States of America

CPSIA compliance information: Batch #CW11GS: For further information contact Gareth Stevens, New York, New York at 1-800-542-2595.

Table of Contents

Basilisk

WINGS
In some descriptions, the wings were more like those of a dragon than of a bird.

TAIL
The tail was long and snaky and may even have been lined with barbed spines.

EYES
Some say the eyes glowed a fiery red, like hot coals. Whatever their color, they were deadly.

COMB
The bright, pointed cock's comb on the head was said to resemble a king or queen's crown.

BODY
This was rounded like a rooster's but had few feathers. Nobody is really sure how big the monster grew.

SKIN
This was as scaly as the skin of the roughest snake.

BEAK
In many accounts, the beak was lined with dagger-like teeth.

HISS
When the basilisk hissed, serpents fled in terror.

TONGUE
Some people said the basilisk had a forked tongue, like a snake.

CLAWS
The beast ran swiftly on feet that bristled with horrendously sharp claws.

The basilisk was a horrific mix of reptile and bird. It was said to be hatched from a freak egg laid by a cockerel, an egg that was then incubated by a toad. With their snake-like bodies, cockerel heads and stumpy wings, basilisks had terrifying magical powers. Just the stare of a basilisk could kill people, as could its foul, poisonous breath. It polluted waterways and turned green, fertile farmland into nothing but barren desert. Rocks would shatter if the basilisk brushed against them. There were few ways to kill a basilisk. Weasels were said to be immune to basilisk magic and poison, and if a basilisk was confronted with a mirror, it would be killed by its own reflection.

A toad carefully tended a strange egg abandoned in a grassy field. The warty amphibian watched as first cracks, then a hole appear in the shell. Soon a bird-like head popped out—but this is no fluffy, harmless chick. Moments later, the toad keeled over, stone dead. It was the first victim of a new basilisk's deadly gaze.

WHERE IN THE WORLD?

EUROPE

The Roman writer Pliny described the basilisk nearly 2,000 years ago, but the creature may be even older. People throughout Europe walked in terror of meeting it right up until the 16th century, when the famous naturalist Konrad Gesner denounced it as "gossip."

ACTUAL SIZE

DID YOU KNOW?

• In Warsaw in Poland in 1587, a basilisk was blamed for killing two small girls in a cellar. Reportedly, a "volunteer" prisoner sent down into the cellar killed the creature with a mirror.

• The basilisk myth may come from early reports of hooded cobras, venomous Indian snakes that rear up and flare a hood of skin. The idea that a weasel can kill a basilisk may come from tales of the mongoose, a small mammal that preys on cobras.

Catoblepas

EYES
According to the legend, any human who looks into the eyes of this creature will instantly drop dead.

NECK
Its name means "that which looks downward" as its huge head is too heavy for its long, thin neck.

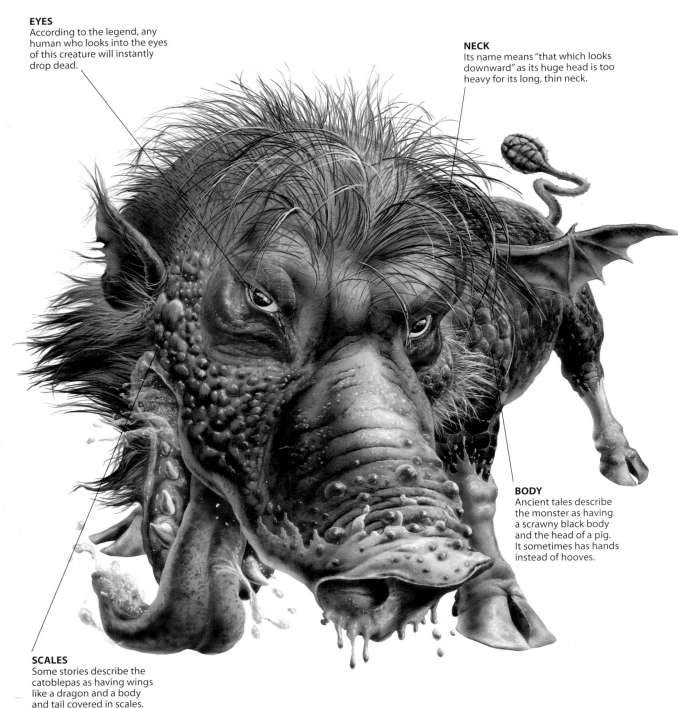

BODY
Ancient tales describe the monster as having a scrawny black body and the head of a pig. It sometimes has hands instead of hooves.

SCALES
Some stories describe the catoblepas as having wings like a dragon and a body and tail covered in scales.

The catoblepas is surprisingly well documented, with Pliny the Elder (a Roman writer and nature scholar) and Leonardo da Vinci among the famous people to describe the creature in their works. Its most notable feature is its heavy head that always hangs down—which is fortunate, for most people thought that its gaze could turn you to stone or, even worse, kill you. Others said that its breath was just as deadly, as the creature ate only poisonous vegetation. It has red eyelids and thinning hair on top, and a long, lolling tongue. Its head is too big for its body.

It is said that there lives a hog-like creature in Ethiopia, near a spring or well that is the source of the great River Nile. This beast is powerful, and is conscious of that power…if it becomes frightened, it will open its mouth and exhale a most sharp and horrible breath, which poisons the air around its head. Any that shall approach without meeting its gaze shall lose their voice and become seized with convulsions. Even the most brave, should they see his red and bloodshot eyes, shall die by turning to stone.

ACTUAL SIZE

WHERE IN THE WORLD?

EGYPT

ETHIOPIA

This unusual creature was said to live in Egypt and Ethiopia, favoring swampy areas or wetlands.

DID YOU KNOW?

• Some travelers described their encounters with the catoblepas, including its enormous pink eyes—which is strange, considering its gaze was supposed to kill a person.

• The nineteenth-century French author Flaubert included the catoblepas as one of the horrors to be endured by the hero in his book, *The Temptation of Saint Anthony.*

• Roleplay games such as Dungeons and Dragons often feature the character of catoblepas. There is also a Monster in My Pocket catoblepas figure and a Yu-Gi-Oh! card featuring Catoblepas and the Witch of Fate.

• In some stories, this creature appears as Katobleps or Katoblepon.

• It is often thought that early travelers may have mistaken the gnu (wildebeest), water buffalo, or even a warthog for some sort of heavy-headed, scaly monster.

Cerberus

TAIL
Even Cerberus's tail is poisonous, making it as dangerous as the three howling heads. A single lash from his snake-like tail is fatal.

HEADS
Cerberus has blood-red eyes, acute hearing, and slobbering mouths lined with 126 razor-sharp teeth.

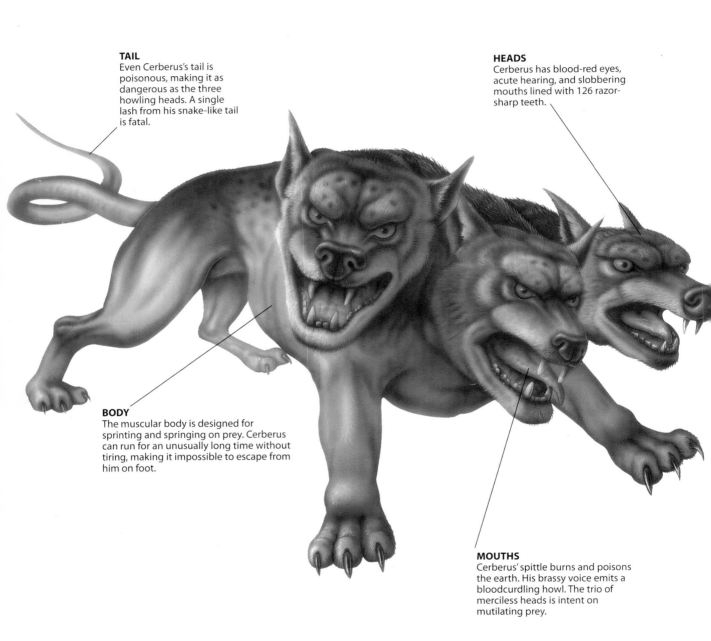

BODY
The muscular body is designed for sprinting and springing on prey. Cerberus can run for an unusually long time without tiring, making it impossible to escape from him on foot.

MOUTHS
Cerberus' spittle burns and poisons the earth. His brassy voice emits a bloodcurdling howl. The trio of merciless heads is intent on mutilating prey.

Cerberus, the three-headed hound with a snake's tail, guards the entrance to the underworld to prevent the living from entering and the dead from escaping. If the dead attempt to escape, they are devoured. Living visitors who attempt to enter the underworld risk the same fate. His watchful eyes, keen hearing, and foul temper make it impossible to sneak past him. Those who do get by him accomplish the task through trickery. Orpheus, one of the best-known musicians in Greek mythology, can charm wild beasts with his songs. Playing a song on his lyre, Orpheus lulls Cerberus to sleep and creeps past to seek his beloved wife.

The hero Hercules was given the task of capturing Cerberus as the last of the 12 labors assigned to him by the king. The rulers of the underworld gave Hercules permission to capture Cerberus on the condition that he did not harm the dog. Hercules wrestled the evil creature into submission using brute strength alone. He seized the dog by two of its throats and hauled the struggling animal out of the underworld. When Hercules brought Cerberus out of Hades, the king was so frightened that he hid in a large storage jar.

ACTUAL SIZE

WHERE IN THE WORLD?

GREECE

Cerberus stands guard at the entrance to Hades, the underworld of Greek mythology, which is populated by the dead.

DID YOU KNOW?

• Once Hercules proved to the king that he could capture Cerberus, he returned the terrible dog to his post in Hades.

• The name Cerberus means "demon of the pit."

• Hades, the land of the dead in Greek mythology, lies beneath the ground. The River Styx is the boundary between the underworld and the earth. The Styx represents hate and is said to wrap around Hades nine times. Cerberus, feared by the gods themselves, can be found guarding the gates of Hades.

• Poisonous plants sprout from the foam that drips from his trio of snarling mouths.

Chimera

HEADS
With three mouths to feed, the Chimera is always hungry. The serpent head, the lion head, and the goat head sometimes torch their prey before eating it. More often than not, they consume their terrified victims alive.

BODY
Part lion, part goat, the Chimera has an impenetrable hide that cannot be pierced by sword or spear.

REAR LEGS
The rear legs of a goat give the Chimera uncanny agility. It scrambles easily over all types of terrain in search of a target for its rage.

JAWS
The Chimera's mighty jaws spew forth a ferocious stream of fire that converts forests into kindling, homes into smoking ruins, and crops into useless ash.

FRONT LEGS
The powerful forelegs of a lion are necessary to support the Chimera's three hulking heads. Its claws are handy for ripping flesh it has not already gulped down or roasted.

The ghastly Chimera, once the pet of the king of Caria, escapes. Rampaging within the king's court, it terrorizes everyone it meets with its three fearsome heads: the head of a goat, the head of a lion, and the head of a serpent. Continually vomiting flames, it ravages the countryside and sets fire to everything in sight. When the Chimera reaches Lycia, it sears the land with its fiery breath and consumes every living thing that crosses its path. Not only is the beast swift footed and strong, it is immortal as well. No weapon made by humans can harm it.

Bellerophon, one of the greatest heroes of Greek mythology, was sent by the king of Lycia to slay the Chimera. Riding his winged horse Pegasus, courageous Bellerophon flew high above the Chimera's searing flames. The monster's breath was hot enough to melt the hero's spear, so Bellerophon placed a block of lead on the tip of his spear. He flew straight at the beast and thrusted the lead-tipped spear into the Chimera's throat. Its flaming breath melted the lead, which sealed the Chimera's throat shut. The Chimera quickly suffocated.

ACTUAL SIZE

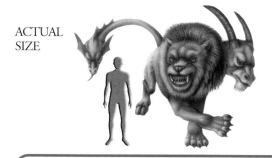

WHERE IN THE WORLD?

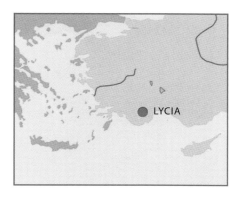

LYCIA

Residents of ancient Lycia, which lies on the southwestern coast of modern-day Turkey, lived in fear of the fire-breathing Chimera.

DID YOU KNOW?

• The Chimera claims both the Hydra and Cerberus as its siblings. Their parents specialized in producing monstrous beasts with multiple heads.

• Athena, the warrior goddess, gave Bellerophon a golden bridle in a dream as he slept in her temple. Waking to find the bridle still in his hands, he used it to capture Pegasus, the winged horse he would ride to face the Chimera.

• Lycia was once a happy place, but the inhabitants lived with the constant fear that they or a loved one would be snatched up and consumed by the Chimera.

• In some accounts, the Chimera has the head of a lion, the body of a goat, and the tail of a snake.

Echidna

TAIL
The lower half of her body is that of a snake. It is not clear whether she slithered along the ground, or was able to hold herself upright.

WINGS
In some ancient paintings, she is shown as having wings or having a tail that is split into two serpent tails.

BODY
Echidna has the body and head of a beautiful woman, to help entice her victims into her company.

BEAUTY
She may not sound too gorgeous, with a tail instead of legs, but the ageless beauty of her face makes men blind to her lower half.

This vicious snake woman, whose name means "she viper," lives in a cave and uses her beauty and charm to lure men to their doom. It is said that she only comes out of the cave far enough to keep her tail end hidden. Once a man falls for her and enters her cave, she grabs him in a death embrace and eats him. Echidna is said to never grow old—which may explain how she has so many children. She is also supposed to be immortal but is finally killed off while she sleeps by the hundred-eyed giant Argus.

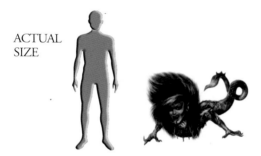

ACTUAL SIZE

Echidna was aptly named the "Mother of all Monsters" who, together with her partner Typhon and her son Orthrus, spawned a great number of the horrible creatures that are featured in Greek myths. She was supposedly the creator of Cerberus (the dog of the underworld), Chimera (the fire-breathing goat–lion–serpent crossbreed), the Nemean Lion, Hydra (a serpent with nine heads), as well as various Harpies, dragons, Sphinx, dogs, an eagle, a fox, and a sow. She is also supposed to have had four children by Hercules, including a sea monster called Scylla.

WHERE IN THE WORLD?

SCYTHIA

Mythology has Echidna living in Scythia, an area of Europe and Asia occupied by the Scythians between 800 BC and AD 200.

DID YOU KNOW?

• Echidna met and trapped Hercules by stealing his horses while he slept. When he awoke, she struck a bargain with him. He could have his horses back as long as he lived with Echidna for a while.

• Don't get her confused with the small, spiny Australian animal, the echidna.

• Echidna is often described as furious and cunning. Despite being blessed with immortality, and not ever looking older, she is angry at the world and intent on destroying mankind.

• Also spelt Ekhidna, she represents or rules over all the corruptions of the earth, such as illness and disease, rot, slime, and stagnant, fetid waters, sea scum, and fetid salt marshes.

Erymanthian Boar

SIZE
The Erymanthian boar is a beast of giant proportions, bigger than a man. The ground shakes when it passes by.

FUR
Unlike a domestic pig, the boar is a long-haired, shaggy-coated wild animal.

TUSKS
An ordinary boar's tusks are large, pointed, and dangerous, so you can imagine how huge and ferocious this monster's tusks are.

JAWS
The boar strikes fear in the hearts of local villagers when they see its foaming jaws looming at them.

This mighty boar is named after its mountain home, for it lives on Mount Erymanthus in Arcadia. It has a reputation for raiding local farms and clearing the fields of crops. If it is still hungry, then it goes on the rampage for the village residents to fill its boarish belly. The great beast strikes fear in the heart of everyone around it, but no one can kill it or even capture it. That is, until King Eurystheus challenges Hercules to seek out the boar as one of his 12 labors. His task is to not only find the boar, but catch it and take it back alive.

It was a long journey to Mount Erymanthus, and along the way Hercules stopped and ate with his friend Phlos the centaur. An accident led to the death of Phlos, and the rage within Hercules drove him on to find the giant boar. He came across it in the forests and chased it up the snow-covered mountain. As it ran and ran it grew weaker, and eventually fell into a snowdrift. Hercules tied it up by its ankles and—being the strongest man in the world—carried it back to Eurystheus.

ACTUAL SIZE

WHERE IN THE WORLD?

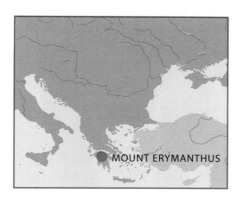

MOUNT ERYMANTHUS

Mount Erymanthus is in southern Greece, and is the fourth tallest mountain in the Peloponnese peninsula.

DID YOU KNOW?

• Hercules has to complete his 12 labors to make up for murdering his wife and two children. He did this while cursed by madness from the goddess Hera, who hated Hercules.

• Some storytellers suggest that Hercules discussed his task with Phlos before the centaur died, and it was his idea to slow down the boar by chasing it into the thick snow.

• When Hercules presented the boar to King Eurystheus, the King was so frightened that he hid in his own bronze wine jar.

Geryon and Orthrus

WINGS
In some pictures, Geryon has four wings in addition to the extra heads, bodies, and arms.

HEADS
Thanks to a curse on his grandmother, Geryon has three heads, three bodies, and three sets of arms.

HOUND
Orthrus is a hellhound—an enormous, two-headed dog that bred with his mother to produce other monsters such as the Sphinx.

Geryon is a three-for-the-price-of-one monster giant. Variously described with three heads, three bodies, or three sets of legs, he is one thing for sure: a huge, monstrous meanie. As if a three-headed giant isn't enough, Geryon is kept company by a two-headed hound, Orthrus. This dog is the brother of the three-headed monster mutt, Cerberus (and so the offspring of Echidna) and is helped in the guarding of the cattle by a giant called Eurytion. The cattle were famous far and wide, and known for their magnificent coats that were tinged red by the sunset.

Geryon and his red cattle are important in the stories of Hercules (sometimes called Heracles), the son of the supreme god, Zeus. One of Hercules' 12 labors, or tasks, was to capture the cattle of Geryon. He sailed in a golden goblet given to him by the sun god Helios, and fought off Orthrus and Eurytion with a giant club. As he tried to escape with the cattle, Geryon attacked him, so Hercules had to finish him off with his bow and a set of poisonous arrows.

ACTUAL
SIZE

DID YOU KNOW?

• **Geryon has associations with the constellation Orion, which is unusual as it can be seen in both the northern and southern hemispheres. The nearby dog constellations Canis Major and Canis Minor are linked to the two-headed Orthrus.**

• **Some tales allow Geryon a single body, but give him three heads and three sets of legs. In others, he has three heads on a single set of shoulders, and no extra limbs at all. Confusing!**

• **The gorgon Medusa, with snakes for hair and a petrifying gaze, was Geryon's grandmother. Her daughter, Chrysaor, sprung from Medusa's beheaded body and later gave birth to Geryon.**

• **On his journey to Erythia, Hercules divided a mountain. The two parts became known as the Pillars of Hercules, and left the Strait of Gibraltar between Spain and Morocco.**

WHERE IN THE WORLD?

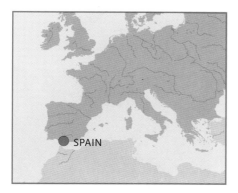

SPAIN

Geryon kept his cattle on the island of Erythia, thought to be in modern-day southern Spain.

Gorgon

WINGS
Each of the three gorgons has golden wings with enormous claws. The wings can be heard as they move around, making an unnerving rattling noise.

HAIR
Instead of beautiful locks of hair, a gorgon has a mass of tangled snakes with vicious fangs writhing around her head.

EYES
People lived in fear of the gorgons and said that anyone they looked upon would be turned instantly to stone.

BLOOD
The blood of a gorgon was a powerful substance, believed to be either poisonous or have magical powers that could bring the dead back to life.

GORGON

In classic mythology, there are three gorgon sisters, Medusa, Stheno, and Euryale. Medusa is mortal, allowing Perseus to track her down and cut off her head, but the other two are immortal. The gorgons are eternally linked to the ocean, seen as storm demons who drag sailors to their death on the submerged rocks and corals of the deep. Their most famous attribute is their power to turn their victim to stone, either by looking at him, or by him looking at them.

ACTUAL SIZE

To find the three gorgons, Perseus first had to find their three sisters, the Graeae or Grey Women. They lived in a cave where they shared one eye and one tooth between them. When he found the cave, they were passing their eye from sister to sister so each could see for a short time. Perseus grabbed the eye from them and refused to give it back until they told him where to find the gorgons. As he approached the gorgons' cave, he could see crumbling statues scattered everywhere: previous victims of the sisters' deathly, stony stare.

WHERE IN THE WORLD?

HYPERBOREA

The gorgons were believed to live in the Greek paradise of the Hyperboreans, in the northern parts of Europe.

DID YOU KNOW?

• In ancient tales, Homer told of just a single gorgon, a monster of the underworld. Later on, the Greek poet Hesiod talked about three gorgon sisters, the offspring of the sea god Phorcys and his wife Ceto.

• Many pieces of ancient Greek art and architecture feature the striking head of a gorgon. Plaques above doorways were believed to prevent evil from entering a home, and shields with a gorgon's head helped prevent losses in battle.

• The Greeks probably got their tales of the snake-haired gorgons from an ancient Libyan religion in which a trio of wise goddesses had snakes for hair, because snakes represented wisdom.

Griffin

WINGS
Although the male griffin is often described as wingless, the female has wings like a great eagle. In some tales she flies like a bird, but in others, she only takes to the air with short hops when fighting.

EARS
Early Mesopotamian images show the griffin with a crested head, but in later pictures it has feathered, pointed ears.

HEAD
The griffin usually has an eagle's head, with terrible piercing eyes and a sharp, curving beak.

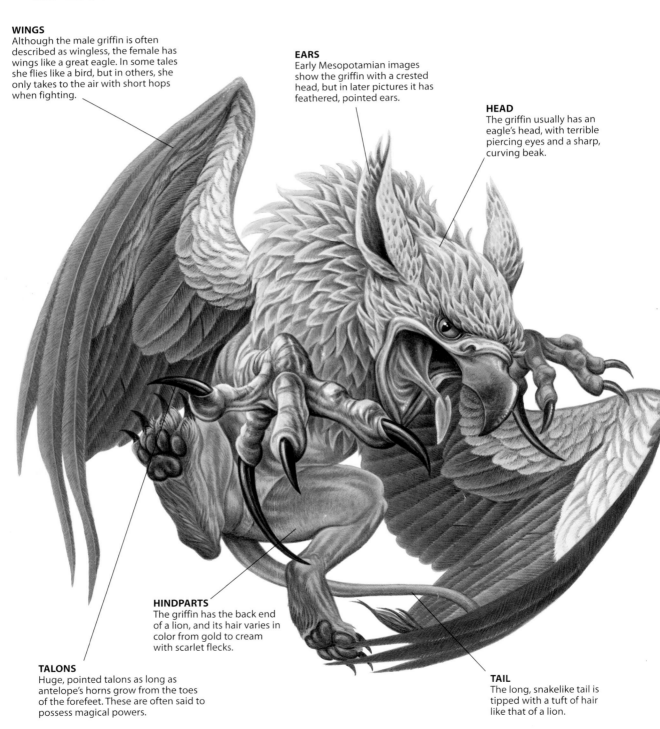

HINDPARTS
The griffin has the back end of a lion, and its hair varies in color from gold to cream with scarlet flecks.

TALONS
Huge, pointed talons as long as antelope's horns grow from the toes of the forefeet. These are often said to possess magical powers.

TAIL
The long, snakelike tail is tipped with a tuft of hair like that of a lion.

This ferocious mythological beast has the head, wings, and forelegs of an eagle, and the hindquarters of a lion. Given to attacking other animals at will, it's also said to tear up humans on sight with its slashing claws and tearing beak. The griffin is a colossally powerful predator that can carry off a yoke of oxen in its claws—in some medieval accounts, it is stronger than 8 lions and 100 eagles. It also hoards gold and emeralds, fiercely attacking anyone who tries to steal from its nest.

Many griffins were said to live in the ancient land of Scythia, north of the Black Sea—an area rich in gold and jewels. Digging up these treasures with their claws, they used them to line their nests. The Arimaspians wanted these riches, too, and often rode on horseback into battle with the griffins. As a result, griffins attacked horses whenever they could. Gripping with their scythe-like claws, they hacked in with the hooked bill, leaving terrible, bloody wounds.

WHERE IN THE WORLD?

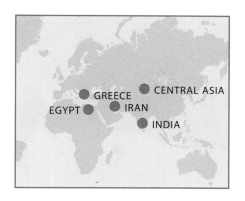

GREECE
CENTRAL ASIA
EGYPT
IRAN
INDIA

Griffins were thought to live in various parts of the Near and Middle East, from Egypt, Greece, and Turkey through to Syria, Iraq, Iran, and Armenia. They were also strongly associated with India and southern parts of central Asia.

ACTUAL SIZE

DID YOU KNOW?

• Artifacts from ancient Greece sometimes show the griffin with a mane of tightly coiled curls.

• One Norse legend tells of Prince Hagen, who was carried away to a griffin's nest. Fortunately, he found a suit of armor and managed to kill the young griffins as they attacked.

• The female griffin lays eggs like those of an eagle.

Harpy

FACE
The harpy has the face of an ugly old hag, with pointed ears and a long warty nose.

HAIR
Straggly, matted hair is coated with dirt, just like the rest of the creature.

TALONS
Each scaly finger and toe is armed with a sharp brass talon.

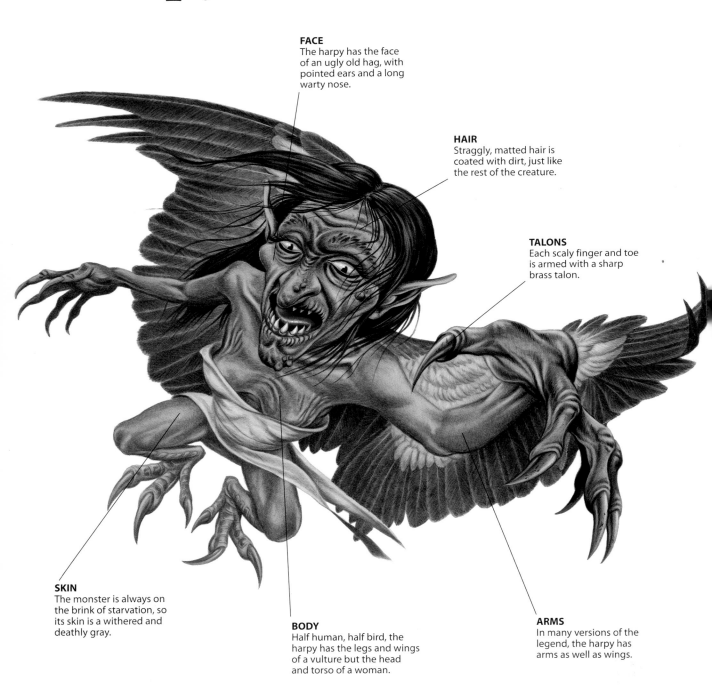

SKIN
The monster is always on the brink of starvation, so its skin is a withered and deathly gray.

BODY
Half human, half bird, the harpy has the legs and wings of a vulture but the head and torso of a woman.

ARMS
In many versions of the legend, the harpy has arms as well as wings.

Reeking of dirt and decay, these ghastly females have the body and head of a screeching hag and the wings and tail of a scavenging vulture. They leave a horrible stench wherever they go. The harpies first appeared in Greek legend, and they were linked with the terrifying power of storms and gales. They were also believed to carry off the souls of the dead, transporting them to the underworld.

ACTUAL SIZE

In exchange for his eyesight, King Phineus had accepted from Zeus the power to see into the future. But later, the king offended Zeus by giving away the gods' secret plans. In punishment, Zeus sent the harpies to plague him for all time. Their thieving habits doomed the king to an eternity of awful hunger. A visit from the Argonauts finally saved blind Phineus. The roving Greek heroes promised to help him in return for his advice. Phineus threw a lavish banquet, and soon the harpies swooped screeching from the skies, circling the table and grabbing handfuls of food. Two of the Argonauts, Zetes and Calais, had powerful wings. They drew their weapons and flew after the harpies, chasing them away.

WHERE IN THE WORLD?

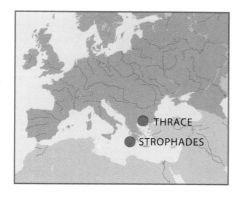

- THRACE
- STROPHADES

Classical legends say that the harpies were expelled from Thrace by the Argonauts. They were forced to take permanent refuge on a group of islands in the Ionian Sea, west of Greece, which later became known as the Strophades.

DID YOU KNOW?

• Although the harpy is constantly hungry and is always on the verge of starvation, it is an immortal being, incapable of ever dying.

• Legend says when the harpies fled from Thrace, one fell exhausted into a river in the Peloponnese in Greece.

• In some versions of the harpy myth, these monsters have the claws of a lion and the ears of a bear.

• The harpy has a namesake that lives in the tropical forests of South America: the harpy eagle. This rare, giant bird of prey has a menacing beak and deeply curved talons. It is powerful enough to snatch sloths and monkeys from the treetops.

• Four harpies appear in some stories. Translated, their names mean "rain squall," "storm dark," "swift flying," and "swift foot."

Hecatonchires

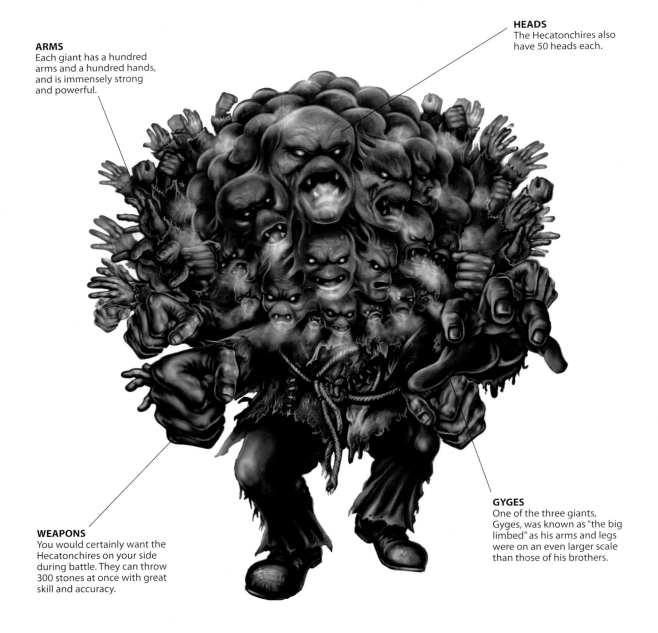

HEADS
The Hecatonchires also have 50 heads each.

ARMS
Each giant has a hundred arms and a hundred hands, and is immensely strong and powerful.

WEAPONS
You would certainly want the Hecatonchires on your side during battle. They can throw 300 stones at once with great skill and accuracy.

GYGES
One of the three giants, Gyges, was known as "the big limbed" as his arms and legs were on an even larger scale than those of his brothers.

The Hecatonchires are giants from Greek mythology, and there are usually three of them. They get their name (and their Roman name, Centimanes) from their distinguishing feature. It means "hundred handed." The three brothers are the original sons of Gaia (creator of the Earth) and Uranus (god of the sky) and are called Gyges the Big Limbed, Briareus the Vigorous, and Cottus the Furious. Each of them is powerful enough to lift and throw mountains.

ACTUAL SIZE

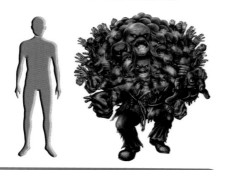

When the Hecatonchires were born, their father was so disgusted at the sight of them that he threw them into the darkness of Tartarus, part of the underworld and a place of punishment surrounded by three walls. They were guarded by a dragon until their mother asked Zeus to rescue them. In return, they fought for Zeus against the Titans, who soon surrendered. The Hecatonchires were then given the job of guarding the Titans in Tartarus.

WHERE IN THE WORLD?

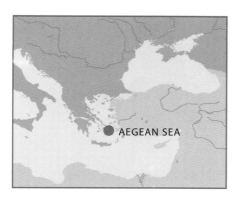

AEGEAN SEA

After guarding Tartarus, the giants were given homes in the River Okeanos (which encircled the whole Earth) and the Aegean Sea near Greece.

DID YOU KNOW?

• These giants were also the brothers of the Cyclopes (one-eyed giants) and the Titans (rulers of the world after overthrowing their father). The Hecatonchires and Cyclopes were responsible for earthquakes, tidal waves, hurricanes, and thunder and lightning.

• In one version of the story, the three giants were so hideous that their father tried to push them back inside their mother as if they were never born. Not surprisingly, this upset Gaia and caused her such pain that she swore revenge on Uranus.

• Briareus had two different names. The gods called him Briareus, but on Earth he was known as Aigaion or Aegaeon, the "Sea goat", and the Aegean Sea was named after him.

Hydra

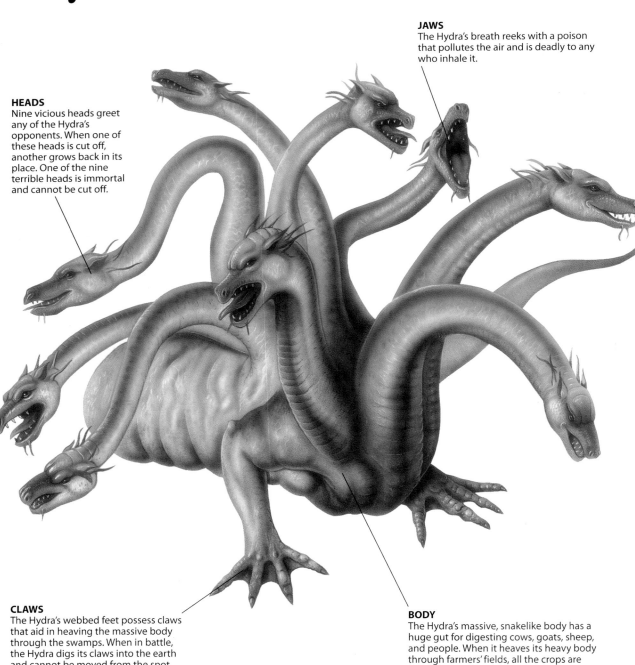

JAWS
The Hydra's breath reeks with a poison that pollutes the air and is deadly to any who inhale it.

HEADS
Nine vicious heads greet any of the Hydra's opponents. When one of these heads is cut off, another grows back in its place. One of the nine terrible heads is immortal and cannot be cut off.

CLAWS
The Hydra's webbed feet possess claws that aid in heaving the massive body through the swamps. When in battle, the Hydra digs its claws into the earth and cannot be moved from the spot.

BODY
The Hydra's massive, snakelike body has a huge gut for digesting cows, goats, sheep, and people. When it heaves its heavy body through farmers' fields, all the crops are crushed and destroyed.

Ancient Lerna conceals an entrance to the underworld, which is guarded by the terrible, nine-headed Hydra. Its poisonous breath fouls the air with a stench strong enough to kill a man. The Hydra also ranges through the countryside, flattening crops and terrifying locals. Neither livestock nor citizens are safe from the beast with nine ravenous heads. If any one of its heads is cut off, another immediately grows back in its place. Many people die of fright just from the sight of the Hydra.

Everyone in Lerna believed that the Hydra could not be destroyed until the arrival of Hercules, who was determined to kill the menace. Hercules fired flaming arrows into the Hydra's lair to draw it out into the open. He began chopping off Hydra heads with his sword, only to discover that they grew back as fast as he could lop them off. With a flaming torch in hand, Hercules's nephew came to his aid by scorching the wound as soon as Hercules cut off a head. When burned, the heads could not grow back. However, one of the Hydra's heads is immortal and cannot be removed by any weapon that a person can make.

ACTUAL SIZE

WHERE IN THE WORLD?

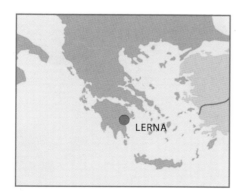

LERNA

The Hydra could be found in the swamps and lake near the ancient city of Lerna in Argolis, Greece.

DID YOU KNOW?

• To kill the Hydra's one immortal head, Hercules crushes its skull with an enormous club and then rips off the head with his bare hands. He buries the head beneath a large rock, where it can no longer trouble anyone.

• Hercules dips his arrowheads in the Hydra's poisonous blood, making them lethal.

• When Hercules approaches the Hydra, he covers his mouth and nose with a cloth to avoid inhaling its lethal fumes.

• Killing the Hydra was the second of 12 tasks the king assigned to Hercules. The king sat on the throne originally intended for Hercules.

• The Hydra's siblings are the Chimera and Cerberus.

Lamia

HEAD
Lamia has a human head with the face of a beautiful young woman. She was so attractive that Zeus, the most important of the Greek gods, fell in love with her.

EYES
She is cursed to have her eyes permanently open, but later Zeus grants her the power to pluck out her own eyeballs to relieve her from the torture of images of her lost children.

TEETH
With her mouth closed, Lamia is a beautiful temptress. Look inside, though, and you'll see the vicious teeth she needs to devour young children.

BODY
The top half of Lamia's body takes human form. The bottom half is the golden-speckled body of a snake or serpent.

Is Lamia a monster, a woman, a vampire, or a witch? Tales are told that combine all of these. Commonly, she is a demon who roams at night, invading households to drink the blood of children. Sometimes she steals children from their beds. It may be that she was transformed into a half human, half serpent by her grief over the death of her children. In some cultures she is linked to Lilith, a night demon who can appear as an owl and disturbs people in their sleep. She can bring upsetting dreams and even disease and illness.

Never fall in love with somebody who is already married—especially if he is a Greek god with a jealous wife. Zeus may have had children with Lamia, and his wife Hera was furious and swore revenge. She killed Lamia's children and condemned her to a life with no sleep. Unable to close her eyes, Lamia could never escape the vision of her dead sons and daughters. Her only comfort was to hunt down other people's offspring and take out her torment on them.

ACTUAL SIZE

WHERE IN THE WORLD?

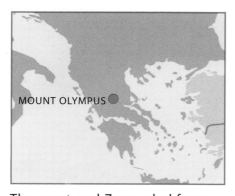

MOUNT OLYMPUS

The great god Zeus ruled from Mount Olympus in ancient Greece, north of Athens. Tales of Lamia are told worldwide to tame disobedient children.

DID YOU KNOW?

• Later versions of Lamia describe her as drinking the blood of any human whether they are children or adults.

• Poets and artists from the romantic movement of the late eighteenth and early nineteenth centuries depict Lamia as a blood-sucking monster who can take the form of a beautiful woman. She has an ordinary body but is often shown with snakeskin adornments.

• In one story, Lamia is daughter of the sea god Poseidon and appears as a shark. In others, where she is portrayed as a beautiful she-demon, she starts life as a Libyan queen.

• Lilith appears in Jewish tales and in the King James version of the Bible. Stories name her as Adam's first wife, before Eve.

Medusa

HAIR
Her long, lustrous hair changes into a slithering mass of poisonous snakes. Any person who manages to approach Medusa without looking at her is still in danger from the aggressive snakes that strike at anything that moves.

FACE
She once stunned men with her striking looks. After the goddess Athena punishes Medusa and turns her into a shocking monster, her cold, frightful gaze stuns them to death.

MOUTH
Medusa's breath has a foul odor similar to the scent of decaying flesh. Her white teeth narrow to points, like a snake's fangs. If anyone manages to get near her without dying, her teeth are capable of flaying the flesh from human bones.

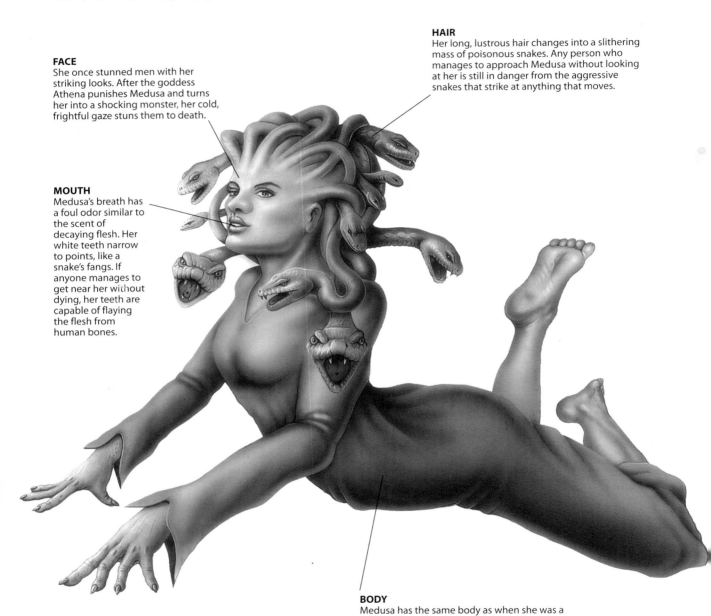

BODY
Medusa has the same body as when she was a beauty. However, with one well-aimed blow of Perseus's mighty sword, her body and terrible head part ways forever.

The only mortal gorgon sister, Medusa was once a beautiful woman. A jealous goddess transformed her into one of the most dangerous creatures imaginable. The god Poseidon falls in love with the gorgeous Medusa, and meets with her in the temple of the goddess Athena. The goddess is furious that her temple is used for anything other than worship. As punishment, she turns Medusa into a gorgon. Her flowing hair is turned into a nest of writhing snakes, and anyone who gazes at her directly is turned immediately into stone. She uses her still-beautiful face to tempt unwary men into her trap.

 Perseus, who was raised by priests from Athena's temple, promises to bring King Polydectes and Athena the head of Medusa. Perseus quietly creeps up to Medusa as she is sleeping. He uses his polished shield as a mirror because looking directly at her means instant death. With her terrible image reflected in his shield, he swings his sturdy sword and cuts off her head with one powerful blow. Even in death, her severed head has the power to turn anyone who looks upon it to stone.

ACTUAL SIZE

WHERE IN THE WORLD?

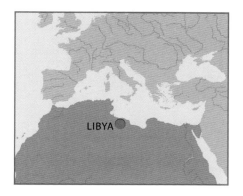

LIBYA

In ancient Libya, on Africa's northern coast, citizens had to be careful not to make eye contact with this ugly, snake-haired lady.

DID YOU KNOW?

• **Perseus places Medusa's head in a pouch and takes it out during battles to turn his enemies to stone.**

• **Medusa's head is later placed on Athena's shield as a symbol of the goddess's power.**

• **When Perseus cuts off Medusa's head, the blood that is spilled creates the multitude of snakes that inhabit Africa to this day.**

• **Medusa's blood changes into red coral when it falls onto the ocean floor.**

• **When King Atlas of Mauritania threatens Perseus and refuses to allow him into his palace, Perseus shows Atlas the severed head of Medusa. At the sight of Medusa's head, King Atlas is changed into a mountain in the desert of Africa. Mount Atlas stands there today, frozen eternally in place.**

Merpeople

LOWER BODY
Instead of legs, a mermaid has a scaly tail like a fish, with a wide fin for powering through the water.

HAIR
These flowing locks are a mermaid's pride and joy. She spends many hours gazing in a silver mirror, combing through the lustrous strands.

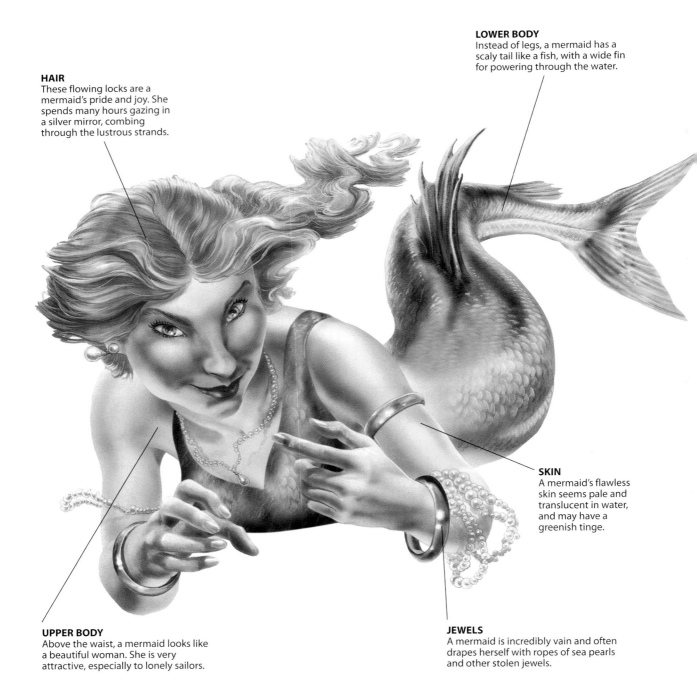

SKIN
A mermaid's flawless skin seems pale and translucent in water, and may have a greenish tinge.

UPPER BODY
Above the waist, a mermaid looks like a beautiful woman. She is very attractive, especially to lonely sailors.

JEWELS
A mermaid is incredibly vain and often drapes herself with ropes of sea pearls and other stolen jewels.

Merpeople are beautiful and elusive creatures, sometimes glimpsed lounging on coastal rocks or swimming through the ocean waves. The earliest stories of these semihuman sea creatures came from ancient Babylon (now in Iraq) about 7,000 years ago. They can also spell disaster for those mariners who see them. Whenever they appear, storms, shipwrecks, and drownings follow close behind. Mermaids, for example, tempt ships onto rocks by bewitching the sailors with their great beauty and haunting songs.

ACTUAL SIZE

A ship had been at sea for several months when the weary sailors found themselves caught in a sudden storm. As their vessel pitched and rolled, the men battened down the hatches and fought to keep their ship afloat, but soon they heard a haunting voice above the noise of the waves. Gradually, they forgot their duties and crowded to the side of the deck, straining to hear the beautiful sound—and the ship drifted inexorably toward some jagged rocks. Catching sight of an alluring female form, the sailors cried out. They seemed oblivious to the danger, until the ship hit the rocks with a savage lurch that jolted several of them overboard. Struggling uselessly against the pounding surf, the last thing each sailor heard before drowning was the evil mermaid laughing delightedly as the ship was torn apart.

WHERE IN THE WORLD?

Merpeople live in all the world's oceans and seas. Sailors usually spot them lounging on rocks along the coast or frolicking out at sea, though a few venture inland by swimming up rivers.

DID YOU KNOW?

• Merpeople are said to hoard vast treasure troves of gold, jewels, and other valuables, which they gather from the hulls of sunken wrecks.

• In the sixth century, legend says a mermaid visited a monk on the remote island of Iona, Scotland, asking for a soul. When the monk demanded that she leave the sea for good, the mermaid left the island crying. Her tears turned into gray-green pebbles that can still be found on the beaches.

• In 1961, the Isle of Man tourist board held a fishing competition where a prize was offered to anyone capturing a mermaid. No one claimed the prize, but there were many reported sightings.

Nemean Lion

MANE
Like all male lions, the Nemean lion has a furry mane around its face to make it look bigger and fiercer. It doesn't need a huge mass of hair, though, as it is very large already.

EYES
One look in this beast's fiery eyes is enough to realize that it means business and shows no mercy to its victims.

SIZE
The monstrous lion is twice the size of any other lion known to man, and has skin so tough that no arrow or sword can pierce it.

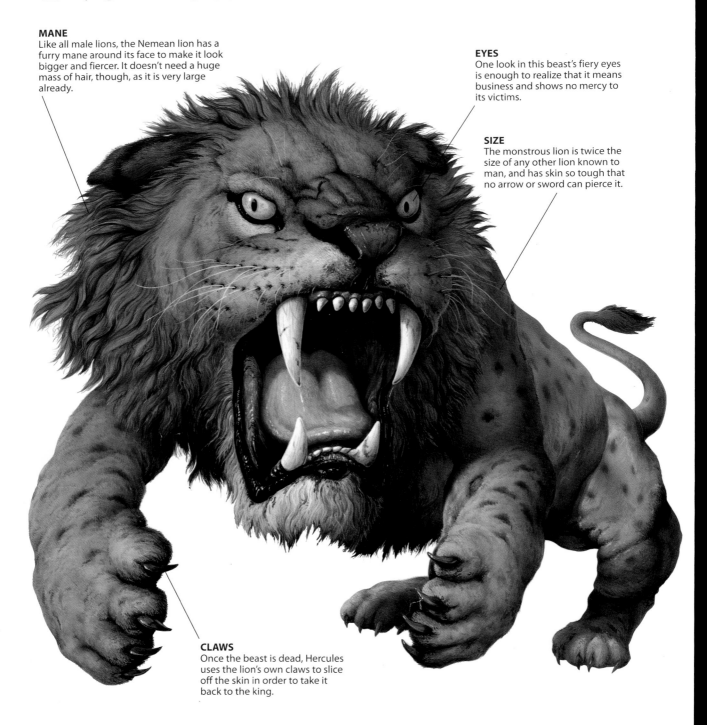

CLAWS
Once the beast is dead, Hercules uses the lion's own claws to slice off the skin in order to take it back to the king.

This lion is one of the enemies to be tackled by Hercules as the first of his 12 labors. The giant lion lives on the Nemean plain, and it is Hercules's first task to kill it and bring back its skin to prove to King Eurystheus that the beast is truly dead. The enormous animal is no ordinary lion but the offspring of the hundred-headed monster Typhon and the half-serpent Echidna. It terrorizes the area of Nemea, gobbling up cattle and humans as it pleases. It is said to be indestructible, and was sent to earth as a plague on the people from the goddess Hera.

Hercules set off armed with his bow and arrow, and a club made by ripping up an olive tree at its roots. He soon realized, when he started to fight the lion, that these ordinary weapons were no use at all. Using his brain, he trapped the beast in its own cave and when it escaped from another exit, he wrestled it to the ground and strangled it using his enormous strength. Even then, he struggled to take the creature's skin as his prize to prove to the king that he had finished his challenge.

ACTUAL SIZE

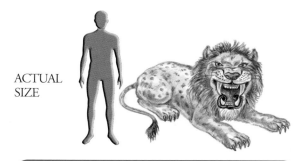

WHERE IN THE WORLD?

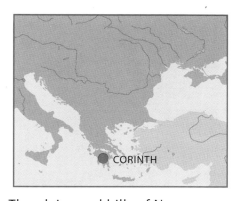

CORINTH

The plains and hills of Nemea are part of the Peloponnese penisula of Greece, near the city of Corinth, which is still there today.

DID YOU KNOW?

• It is usually easy to spot Hercules in ancient paintings, as he is mostly shown wearing the skin of a lion.

• In the myth, when Hercules successfully returns to King Eurystheus, the King is so frightened of Hercules's power that he bans him from the city. He also has a large bronze jar built that he hides in whenever Hercules is near.

• Most of Hercules's stories are represented in the heavens by constellations. This one is Leo the lion.

• Hercules has to give some credit to other people in this task: he only learns that he can skin the lion using its own claws from an old woman passing by (possibly the goddess Athena in disguise).

Scylla

WINGS
Sometimes, Scylla is pictured with wings, but rooted in her cave, she couldn't fly.

NECK
A long, serpentine neck supported each of Scylla's horrible heads, enabling her to reach all the way from her underwater cavern to the ocean surface.

TEETH
Scylla was an avid flesh eater, and easily tore flesh from bone with rows of shark-like teeth.

WAIST
At Scylla's waist, a girdle of ferocious dog's heads snapped and snarled at every passing ship.

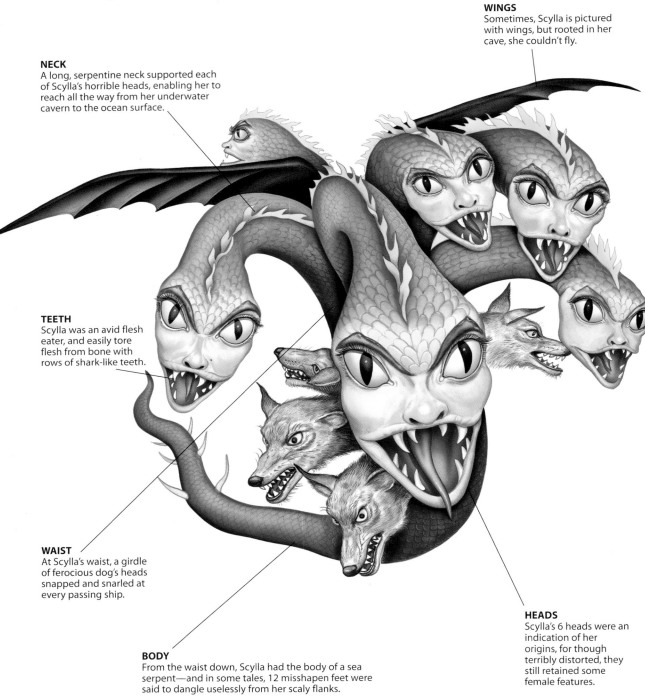

HEADS
Scylla's 6 heads were an indication of her origins, for though terribly distorted, they still retained some female features.

BODY
From the waist down, Scylla had the body of a sea serpent—and in some tales, 12 misshapen feet were said to dangle uselessly from her scaly flanks.

Sailors crossing the narrow strait between Italy and Sicily stood little chance of avoiding Scylla, with her awful shark-toothed jaws and belt of snarling dog heads. She was featured in the epic poem *The Odyssey* by the Greek poet Homer, and in *Metamorphoses* by the Roman poet Ovid. Once a beautiful maiden, she became a foul monster through the magic of the jealous sorceress Circe. She rose from the depths to devour sailors trying desperately to avoid the terrible whirlpool of Charybdis. Hundreds of sailors perished in Scylla's jaws, but her reign of terror ended when Hercules sailed through the strait. Hercules killed her with his club, but Scylla's father restored his wretched daughter's life, and she continued to haunt the strait.

Circe told Odysseus to steer close to the Italian shore as his ship entered the narrow Strait of Messina, and to sail safely around the edge of the raging whirlpool Charybdis. But as soon as he reached the far side, Scylla surged menacingly from her cave. Odysseus was powerless to stop an attack as Scylla's heads reached out and seized several of his best oarsman. All he could do was move on out of danger while the doomed sailors screamed piteously.

WHERE IN THE WORLD?

STRAIT OF MESSINA

Scylla and Charybdis guarded the the Strait of Messina between Italy and Sicily in the Mediterranean. Scylla lay on the Italian side, near the village of Scilla. Charybdis was near Cape Peloro at Sicily's eastern tip.

ACTUAL SIZE

←———328 FEET (100 M)———→

DID YOU KNOW?

• In some versions of the tale, Scylla is eventually turned into a rocky outcrop. This still stands today and is a real danger to passing ships.

• It's possible that Scylla and her snaking heads were based on sailors' tales of giant squid attacking boats.

• Whirlpools still occur in the Strait of Messina, and several historical accounts tell of large naval ships being sucked down to their doom.

Sekhmet

HEAD
The snarling, roaring head of a lion sums up Sekhmet's attitude to fighting and war. She was a terrifying goddess.

HEADDRESS
The disk on her headdress represents the sun. The horns around it are for the cow-headed god Hathor, and the cross with a circle is an ankh, which represents eternal life.

WEAPONS
She has the fearsome teeth and claws of a lioness and can rip a man to shreds and lap up his blood. Her arrows can pierce a person with fire.

BREATH
Sekhmet is the mistress of dread, goddess of the angry sun, and her breath is like the hot desert wind that can destroy any man before her.

This ancient Egyptian goddess is known as the "Eye of Ra," for she was plucked from the head of the sun god Ra. He wanted to teach mankind a lesson for its disobedience to him, and created Sekhmet as his weapon. At first she was made in the form of Hathor, the cow-headed sun goddess. On Earth, though, she became lioness-headed Sekhmet, the warrior goddess, and the angry side of all the good that Hathor represented. She was protector of the gods and her allies, but a fierce enemy to others.

Sekhmet threw herself into battle against the men who had disrespected Ra and ripped them to pieces. Ra, who was not a cruel god, hated what he saw. He was afraid Sekhmet might destroy the whole human race, and so tricked her. He poured red pomegranate juice and beer so that Sekhmet thought it was blood and lapped it up. She became drunk and slept for three days, and when she woke up her rage had faded. Ra set aside a feast day for her and jars of beer and pomegranate juice were offered.

ACTUAL SIZE

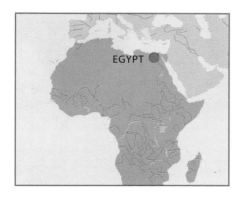

WHERE IN THE WORLD?

EGYPT

Sekhmet was one of about 2,000 gods and goddesses worshipped in ancient Egypt up to 5,000 years ago.

DID YOU KNOW?

• **There are two Egyptian goddesses with lioness heads: Sekhmet, the goddess of the west, often shown wearing red (for the desert), and Bastet, goddess of the east, usually wearing green.**

• **Sekhmet's name comes from the Egyptian "sekhem" which means "to be mighty, strong, and violent."**

• **She is also known as the Lady of Pestilence (which means plague or disease) and was thought to be able to infect any tribe or person who made her angry. On the flip side, she was the goddess of doctors and healers and could cure disease for her allies.**

• **To keep Sekhmet happy, the Egyptians worshiped her with more than 700 statues. Priests had to perform a ritual before a different statue every morning and afternoon, on every day, year after year.**

Siren

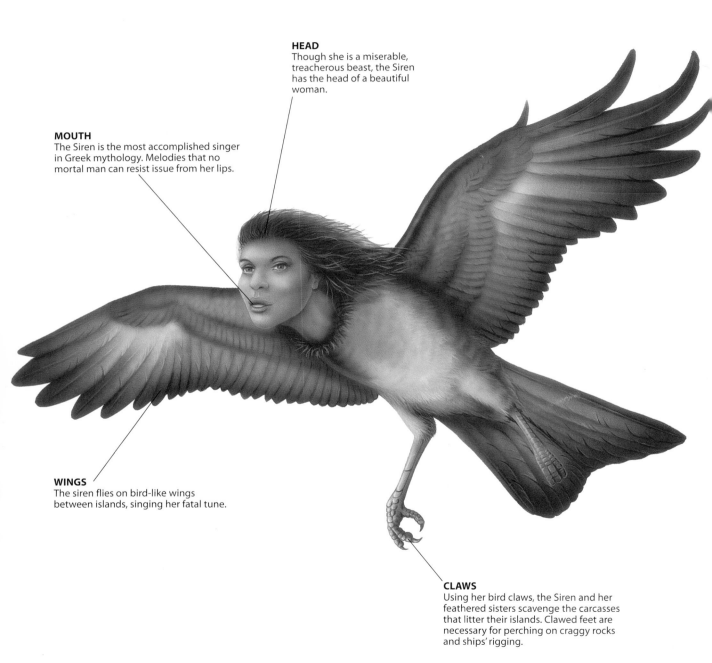

HEAD
Though she is a miserable, treacherous beast, the Siren has the head of a beautiful woman.

MOUTH
The Siren is the most accomplished singer in Greek mythology. Melodies that no mortal man can resist issue from her lips.

WINGS
The siren flies on bird-like wings between islands, singing her fatal tune.

CLAWS
Using her bird claws, the Siren and her feathered sisters scavenge the carcasses that litter their islands. Clawed feet are necessary for perching on craggy rocks and ships' rigging.

Sailors passing by the three rocky islands off the coast of Italy sometimes hear tunes so haunting and sweet that they forget their homes, grow helpless, and crash their ships on the rocks. The musicians are the Sirens, three bird-women who lure sailors to death with their songs. Their islands appear white from the heaps of sun-bleached bones of sailors long ago lured to their doom. Orpheus, the father of songs and inventor of the lyre in Greek mythology, survived the Siren song. Sailing past their islands, he played his lyre so loudly that he drowned out their melody. One sailor heard their song and plunged overboard, but he was saved before he could be tempted toward his own death.

Odysseus grew curious about the Siren's song. He ordered the crew aboard his ship to stuff their ears with beeswax so that they could not be mesmerized to death. Odysseus himself was strapped to the mast of his ship, ensuring that he could hear the Sirens singing but would not be able to throw himself overboard. When he heard their bewitching song, he ordered his crew to untie him, but they could not hear his order. The ship sailed on out of range of their song and all aboard were safe.

ACTUAL SIZE

DID YOU KNOW?

• **Prophecy stated that the Sirens were fated to die when a sailor who hears their song passes unharmed. When Odysseus survived hearing them sing, the Sirens flung themselves into the sea and drowned.**

• **The Sirens sing their beautiful song while swooping through the air or while standing on their islands among the rotting corpses of men they lured to destruction.**

• **In classical art, Sirens are sometimes depicted as women with the wings and legs of birds. In some paintings, they are shown as mermaids playing the lyre or flute.**

• **Li Galli, the islands of the Sirens, were once known as Le Sirenuse in honor of the Sirens.**

WHERE IN THE WORLD?

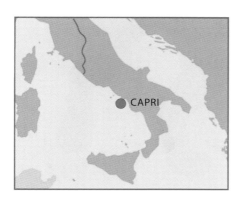

CAPRI

According to Greek myth, the Sirens make their home on three rocky islands called Li Galli. Ancient sailors passing east of the island of Capri, off the southwestern coast of Italy, had to beware.

Sphinx

WINGS
Large eagle's wings enable the Sphinx to swoop down upon anyone answering her riddle incorrectly. After devouring a human, she flies back to her perch and awaits her next victim.

HEAD
An Egyptian headdress and false beard are a remnant of the Sphinx's origins in Egypt, where sphinxes were guardians representing the power of the pharaoh.

BODY
Her robust lion's body gives the Sphinx speed, stealth, and unbelievable strength for pinning her victims.

PAWS
The Sphinx stands on her victim's neck with her mighty lion's paws and chokes the life from him. Sharp claws rake the flesh easily from the human body.

A demon of death, destruction, and bad luck, the Sphinx sits high atop a rock and poses a riddle to all young men who pass by. Those who cannot answer correctly are killed and eaten. This winged lion with a woman's head swoops down and pounces upon her victim. Her riddle is: "Which creature has one voice but goes on four feet in the morning, two feet at noon, and three feet in the evening?" When the Sphinx slaughters King Creon's son, Creon offers his kingdom and the hand of his sister Jocasta in marriage to anyone who can answer the Sphinx's riddle.

Oedipus arrived on the scene and faced the Sphinx. She recited her riddle to Oedipus and readied herself to pounce upon him, but he answers, "A man. In childhood, he crawls on his hands and knees; in adulthood, he walks upright; in old age, he uses a cane." Furious that he has answered her riddle correctly, the Sphinx flung herself from her high perch and died when she landed on the jagged rocks below. Oedipus was awarded Jocasta as his bride, and it was then that his troubles begin.

ACTUAL SIZE

WHERE IN THE WORLD?

EGYPT

The Sphinx originally came from the ancient kingdom of Egypt, dating from the third millenium BC. The Greek hero Oedipus encountered the Sphinx while on his travels.

DID YOU KNOW?

• An oracle predicts Oedipus will kill his father and marry his mother. His father fears the prophecy and abandons Oedipus. Oedipus grows up not knowing he is adopted. On the road one day, Oedipus kills a man during an argument, unaware that the man is his father. Later he marries Jocasta, not knowing she is his mother.

• A plague falls upon the people of Thebes as punishment for having a king and queen who are son and mother. When Oedipus finds out the terrible truth about his parents, he blinds himself. It seems the cursed Sphinx has had her revenge after all.

• Other varieties of sphinxes resemble ram-headed lions or hawk-headed lions.

• The Sphinx's name is derived from a Greek word that means "to strangle."

Basilisk

Area: Europe

Features: A mix of reptile and bird; the head of a rooster; dagger-like teeth in its beak; eyes glow red; forked tongue; sharp claws; scaly skin; long, snaky tail that may have had barbs on it; poisonous breath

Catoblepas

Area: Ethiopia, Egypt

Features: Heavy head of a hog; eyes cause death; long, thin neck that can't hold its head up; poisonous breath

Cerberus

Area: Greece

Features: A three-headed hound with a snake's tail; muscular body; blood-red eyes; spit burns and poisons the earth

Chimera

Area: Lycia

Features: Has three heads, a goat, a lion, and a serpent; rear legs of the goat, front legs of the lion; sharp claws; mouths spew fire; hide cannot be pierced by a sword or spear

Echidna

Area: Scythia

Features: The body and head of a beautiful woman, but her lower half is a snake; sometimes has wings

Erymanthian Boar

Area: Mount Erymanthus

Features: huge, pointed tusks; bigger than a man; shaggy coat; fierce jaws

Geryon and Orthrus

Area: Spain

Features: Geryon is a three-headed giant who is sometimes said to have three bodies and three sets of arms; Orthus is a two-headed dog and Cerberus' brother

Gorgon

Area: Hyperborea

Features: There are three gorgons; have golden wings with claws; snakes for hair; one look at them or from them turns a person to stone; magical blood

Griffin

Area: Greece, Egypt, Iraq, Iran, India, Central Asia

Features: Head, wings, and forelegs of an eagle and the hindquarters of a lion; stronger than 8 lions and 100 eagles; sharp, curving beak; pointed talons that may have magical powers; the female has wings, the male does not

Harpy

Area: Thrace, Strophades

Features: Body and face of a hag; hair coated with dirt; withered, gray skin; legs and wings of a vulture; sharp talons; horrible stench

Hecatonchires
Area: Aegean Sea
Features: Giants with 50 heads, 100 hands; strong enough to lift a mountain

Hydra
Area: Lerna
Features: Nine-headed creature; one head is immortal and cannot be cut off, the others grow back when cut off; huge, snakelike body; poisonous breath kills any who smell it; webbed feet with claws

Lamia
Area: Mount Olympus
Features: Head and torso of a woman, body of a snake; beautiful face; eyes permanently open; teeth able to tear flesh

Medusa
Area: Libya
Features: Snakes for hair; breath smells like decaying flesh; pointy teeth; body of a woman; gaze turns a person to stone; the only mortal gorgon

Merpeople
Area: All oceans and seas
Features: Head and body of a human, lower half of a fish; beautiful hair; skin looks transluscent in water

Nemean Lion
Area: Corinth
Features: Giant lion; furry mane; ferocious eyes; only its own claws can pierce its skin

Scylla
Area: Strait of Messina
Features: Six-headed sea creature; has a belt of dog-heads; shark-like teeth; body of a sea serpent; long necks to support each head; sometimes has wings

Sekhmet
Area: Egypt
Features: Egyptian goddess that has a lioness' head and a woman's body; wears a headdress; very sharp claws and teeth; breath is like hot desert wind and kills

Siren
Area: Capri
Features: Head of a beautiful woman on the body of a bird; sings melodies no mortal can resist, even to his death

Sphinx
Area: Egypt
Features: Winged lion with a woman's head; wears an Egyptian headdress and fake beard; strong body with sharp claws

Glossary

adornment: decoration

cockerel: a young male rooster

cyclops: one-eyed giants of Greek myth

disguise: a change in looks or clothing that hides who you are

elusive: hard to understand

fetid: smelling very bad

hoard: to keep many things to oneself

immortal: endless life

immune: able to withstand

incubate: to keep conditions good for hatching

inexorable: lasting a long time

lustrous: shiny

lyre: a string instrument like a harp

mesmerize: captivate

mutilate: destroy

oracle: a person who a god speaks through

petrify: to turn to stone

piteous: sad

refuge: hiding

scythe: a tool with a curved blade used to cut grass

stagnant: not moving

translucent: see-through

yoke: a wooden frame that connects work animals to a plow

For More Information

Books

Ford, James Evelyn. *The Twelve Labors of Hercules.* Minneapolis, MN: Picture Window Books, 2005.

Levine, Michelle. *Life in Ancient Greece.* Minneapolis: Lerner Press, 2010.

McHargue, Georgess. *The Beasts of Never: A History Natural & Unnatural of Monsters Mythical and Magical.* New York: Delacorte Press, 1988.

Mucci, Tim and Homer. *The Odyssey.* New York: Sterling Publishing, 2009.

Shone, Rob. *Greek Myths.* New York: Rosen Publishing, 2006.

Web Sites

Ancient Greece at the British Museum
www.ancientgreece.co.uk/
Explore Ancient Greece's geography and way of life.

Creature Countdown
animal.discovery.com/tv/a-list/creature-countdowns/mythical/mythical.html
Learn more mythical creatures with Animal Planet's list.

Mythic Creatures
www.amnh.org/exhibitions/mythiccreatures/
Learn about the American Museum of Natural History exhibition.

The Olympic Games
www.perseus.tufts.edu/Olympics/sports.html
Find out about the first Olympic games, which were held in Ancient Greece.

Index